Tess Finds a Seabird

by Isaac Hales
illustrated by Chantal Stewart

Harcourt

SCHOOL PUBLISHERS

Printed in China

ISBN 10: 0-15-351354-3
ISBN 13: 978-0-15-351354-1

Ordering Options
ISBN 10: 0-15-351211-3 (Grade 1 Advanced Collection)
ISBN 13: 978-0-15-351211-7 (Grade 1 Advanced Collection)
ISBN 10: 0-15-358040-2 (package of 5)
ISBN 13: 978-0-15-358040-6 (package of 5)

4 5 6 7 8 9 10   0940   15 14 13 12 11 10 09

Brad and Mom followed their dog, Tess. She was chasing some seaweed that was blowing down the shore. She raced across the sand and pounced on the seaweed.

Then Tess ran to some rocks. She was sniffing the inside of a shell when Brad found her. She pushed the shell around with her nose. She could smell the crab that had lived in it.

Tess found some pools of
water trapped in the rocks. All
of a sudden, her ears went up.
There was a screeching sound
near the cliff.

"What is it, Tess?" whispered
Brad.

"*Yap, yap, yap!*" Tess answered.

Tess ran over to the cliff. She jumped up and down. Brad and Mom ran to see what Tess had found.

"Oh, look, it's a seabird," Mom cried in surprise.

"What *has* it done to get trapped in this net?" asked Brad.

The seabird wouldn't stay still. It struggled to get away, but the net surrounded it. It screeched and screeched.

Brad gazed up and down the shore. Where were the other seabirds? He saw that there were some nests on the cliff face.

"The seabird must have a nest with baby birds up there," said Brad.

"They will be missing their mother," said Mom.

6

Mom bent down and pulled the net off of the seabird. All of a sudden, it flapped its wings. It was free! Off it went, high up in the sky.

Mom, Brad, and Tess sat on the rocks together and watched the seabird. It had flown back to its nest on the cliff. Then they heard some baby birds chirping.

"The seabird and her family will be safe now," said Brad.

"Let's go throw this net in the trash can," said Mom.

"*Yap, yap!*" agreed Tess.